in case of emergency press
We are proud to acknowledge the Traditional Owners
of country throughout Australia and to recognise their
continuing connection to land, waters, and culture.
We pay our respects to their Elders.

We support recognition, reconciliation, and reparation.

A Library of Things

Mark Fleckenstein

in case of emergency press
http://www.icoe.com.au
Travancore, Victoria
Australia

Published by **in case of emergency press** 2022

Copyright © Mark Fleckenstein 2022

All rights reserved. Without limiting the rights under copyright reserved above, no part of this publication may be reproduced, stored in or introduced into a database and retrieval system or transmitted in any form or any means (electronic, mechanical, photocopying, recording or otherwise) without the prior written permission of both the owner of copyright and the above publishers.

ISBN 978-0-6453751-8-3

Acknowledgements

Origami Poem Project: "A Library of Things (Long Version)", "A Library of Things (Short Version)", "Altered Snapshot", "Strictly Personal", "It was Once Called a Nervous Breakdown", "Rote Learning a Dead Language", "Explaining Everything", "Wrong Again and Still Wrong", "A Mirror", "A Theory of Knowledge", "Self Portrait with Wings", "Personal Finance", "The 14th Way of Looking at a Blackbird" and "The Stuff of Dreams Littering the Table"

What Rough Beast: "Experimental Sonnet for Trump's America" and "A Near Sonnet With a Line by C.D. Wright"

Line Break Anthology: "The Secret Life of a Photograph"

Nixes Mate Review: "Recipe Against Despair"

Journal BlazeVOX: "Lamentation (1st Version – 3rd Version)"

Maximus Books: "Rothko's Harvard Murals (Sackler Museum – 11.19.1986)"

Red Ogre: "Self Portrait From a Mirror's Perspective"

"Once there was a man, uncomfortably anonymous the way silence can make a room blush. So went his days, one card at a time, one ticked atop another. And just as quietly and certainly, he became a door. Unlocked, undisturbed by bold paint, infrequently entered or exited."

from 'Handpainted Family Photo Portrait'

Dedication

For g.

Table of contents

A Library of Things	1
A Library of Things (Long Version)	2
The Secret Life of a Photograph	12
Small Poems	**21**
Altered Snapshot	22
Strictly Personal	23
It Was Once Called a Nervous Breakdown	24
Rote Learning a Dead Language	25
Explaining Everything	26
Wrong Again and Still Wrong	27
A Mirror	28
A Theory of Knowledge	29
Self Portrait with Wings	30
Personal Finance	31
The 14th Way of Looking at a Blackbird	32
The Stuff Of Dreams Littering the Table	33
A Catalogue of Poems: Ekphrastic, Recipe, Versions, Experimental, Self Portraits, Epithalamium	**34**
Partial Title of a Photograph	35
Handpainted Family Photo Portrait	38
Rothko's Harvard Murals (Sackler Museum—19th November 1986)	43
Recipe Against Despair	45
Lamentation (1st Version)	46
Lamentation (2nd Version)	47
Lamentation (3rd Version)	48
An Experimental Sonnet for Trump's America	49
A Near Sonnet with a Line by C.D. Wright	50
Self Portrait from a Mirror's Perspective	51
Self Portrait as a Twenty Five-Year Old Question	52
Epithalamium (For Hannah and Kyle)	53
A Library Of Things (Short Version)	54
Notes	**55**
About the Author	**57**

A Library of Things

Mark Fleckenstein

A Library of Things

An unspeakably melancholy memory: I have sometimes traveled for nights on end, down corridors and polished staircases, without coming across a single librarian.

Jorge Luis Borges,
footnote in the short story,
The Library of Babel

A Library of Things (Long Version)

"But she saw him only twice."
"Yes, but that's the beauty of her passion."
                        Henry James, The Turn of the Screw

1.

The soft hours of afternoon begin
to burn. The city skyline opens

its eyes. November, blue-cold. Breath,
frost sheathed conversation.

A thought stands on a terrace, but flesh.
An object, a photograph, a thing.

Blood runs warm through his right arm,
across his wrist, etching small words.

Imagine an impractical room, a looking glass
song, a door neither closed or open.

Startled words, unearthed, rejecting memories.

2.

Today's Horoscope:

When will a truly perfect moment appear,
in which a risk is guaranteed to pay off?

The truth is that right now is as good as it gets.
The stars urge you to leave your fears behind

and jump in wholeheartedly

3.

Wish on the moon, a new moon.
Wish to go back, turn slowly.

Listen slowly, remember, feel,
refine hope. Wishing to make

history just twelve seconds.

4.

The days' held breath exhales
night, the moon, tardy stars,

fists full of darkness.
Heart-pummelled

aspirations faint against the air.

5.

The theory: *make a line drawing
of everywhere you've ever lived,*

and you end up drawing your own face.
The what, was, and where lived.

The mouth and lips practice being geographic.

6.

His disappointed, distracted, damned life,
a dream smeared on an unravelling mirror.

A mirror, empty, age-warped, dusted.
A bruise coloured afterimage.

Incidental, incremental, inchoate, his life.

7.

He talks to himself, confuses word
upon word as longing, desire.

Skin-like callouses map detailed misunderstanding.

8.

Her thought, a sensual grammar,
intimate, like finishing

someone's breath. Her voice,
her words, echolocated

hours later, rub his ears,

9.

The chaos of being human:
nerves, blood, skin, noise.

The sum of our mistakes:
what happens, what will

happen, what has happened.
Chance, the true body,

equal and opposite. Not quite dark, late
afternoon's shrinking habit of light.

Repeated, quieted, slouching, cataclysmic.

10.

When flowers whisper the secret of their fragrance,
what it would be if possible,

may that find you.

The Secret Life of a Photograph

Imagine a looking glass song, memorialized,
mesmerizing. A photograph of a useless

room, a door not closed or open.
Startled words nestled,

beautifully framed, kneeling, spangled with dust.

His breath, an escaped conversation,
the cold makes into icy lace,

a momentary mid-air
decoration. An object

like the photograph he once was.

Delphi: he remembers sitting on
a hill, 6 AM, watching tour buses

slither up the mountain road. Sacred
and profane: an enjambed balance.

What a thing is and exactly what's
missing. The Oracle, never photo-

graphed, readies for seekers.

Wishes on the moon, a new moon, every moon.
Wishes to relive 12 minutes to the second.

Remember: to turn slowly, to feel, not
think. Two words. Hoping to make

the sun rise, even though it already has.

The days' held breath is released.
Night exhales the moon, errant

stars, and paintless darkness. Prayers,
desire, exhausted wishes—wordless,

disembodied, caressed—skulk against the sky.

*If you will know the correct order of letters,
you make a world, you make creation.*

An image and its presumed shadow. How he
talks to himself: shrugs, sighs, muscle pauses,

metastasized longing. An intimate
conversation with absence. Not tactile,

desired. Misunderstanding any means to explain.

A Library of Things Mark Fleckenstein

The theory: *make a line drawing*
of everywhere you've ever lived,

and you'll end up drawing
your own face. Mouth and lips

play at being muscles.

Homecoming: the sum
of our mistakes: skin,

nerves, blood. Nowhere
better than anywhere.

The house rests on its hips.

What he throws his disappeared life
against is hidden: a mirror,

freshly emptied, still wet from
the afterimage. The image

stitched on the back of a mirror.

Small Poems

> I have always believed too much in words.
> **W.S. Merwin**,
> "The Fly"

Altered Snapshot

Hope like photograph, painted unexpectedly
and exactly the right colour.

Strictly Personal

You get to keep the scars. What you do
with them is one way of living.

It Was Once Called a Nervous Breakdown

Not quite crazy, just a few hairs over and away. Not at that hard edge. Time diagnosed, chemically so.

Rote Learning a Dead Language

An excuse for a postcard photo of stars, long absent light-shadows, one blind light-year away.

Explaining Everything

A face crawls off a mirror, scraped free, not wanting to be the mirror's rejected lover.

Wrong Again and Still Wrong

A box defies being made into a gift, nicely wrapped.
The mind empty and whining. And there you are.

A Mirror

1. What It Sees

A mirror's image: not a reflection, but obfuscated thought impersonating a shadow. Afterthought as invention.

2. What It Thinks

The image in a mirror isn't what's been captured but what its plagiarized thought invented.

A Theory of Knowledge

It's not enough to know this morning will empty its pockets of falling snow and rise again, to argue against light.

Self Portrait with Wings

I don't know the world anymore
unfurling his wings.

Personal Finance

Thirty dollars isn't a lifetime but it can be
the stuff of life, dollar contradicting dollar.

The 14th Way of Looking at a Blackbird

When is a blackbird, God's first version of night,
not a blackbird? *Never.*

The Stuff Of Dreams Littering the Table

The question malingering after breakfast, waiting
to be asked again when undressing before bed.

A Catalogue of Poems: Ekphrastic, Recipe, Versions, Experimental, Self Portraits, Epithalamium

"A man sets out to draw the world. As the years go by, he peoples a space with images of provinces, kingdoms, mountains, bays, ships, islands, fishes, rooms, instruments, stars, horses, and individuals. A short time before he dies, he discovers that the patient labyrinth of lines traces the lineaments of his own face."

Jorge Luis Borges,
from *The Aleph and other Stories*

Partial Title of a Photograph
(By Francesca Woodman 3rd April 1958 – 19th January 1981)

1) *Lately I find a sliver of mirror...*

But mirrors don't shed or loosen their skin
after an image disappears. Typically

not named, recalled, thought of, closer to dust,
erasure, disinformation. An escaped soul.

No one wonders what the mirror thinks as they walk away.

2) Lately I find a sliver of mirror...

That was left for me to find. Innocuous.
The way the waxing moon is meant

to hold the sky open as the dark wanes.

3) Lately I find a sliver of mirror...

The size, shape, optical surface of my life.
A last chance, lost change, self-portrait.

Shifts, becomes the portion of the eye,
partially revealing its colour. Resembles

a piece of prayer. Misunderstood, failed, faulty, falling.

Handpainted Family Photo Portrait

1.

Morning. I am
mourning. And years strung together with coughed breath, spit and swear words
dressed in finery, blood cloaked, hand wrung
just like in the movies (clip of a man wringing his hands over and over)
no sound or laugh track. *This is serious.* Years, paper clip impression
to the top left edge. It could
be how paper does an impersonation of a human voice. No,
not the word part, the voice, (the intention, if carried out,
not just the indentation).
But then also somewhere before, and what's possible becomes
overwhelming, indistinctive, obligatory, a photograph of a song.
But also there is a woman, complete, unforeseen as possible.
The same way beauty is possible but also unnecessary.
And she is (beautiful in accordance with current aesthetic principles
and standards).
A thing of beauty to behold, and to be held (caption: male, gender) in
arms.
His.

Specifics? How much wood would a woodchuck chuck if a
woodchuck could chuck wood?
A winter's worth. A household also to be held.
Meaning: beams, joints, studs, drywall, sheetrock, concrete, bricks,
aluminium, iron, stainless steel, plastic, glass, cooper, fiberglass, paint.

The interior (after the door closes), room upon room upon room, etc.,
kitchen, bathroom, living,
bed, cellar, attic, garage, (car inserted),
family.

Family (*Intimate domestic collection of people related by blood*)
Genus (*Homo Sapiens*)
Species (*Culture-bearing Primate*)

Scattered dolls imbibing space, degrees of furniture and divers appliances
for various situations and imparted needs.

Population.

    1)   A man (head)
    2)   A woman (helpmate)
    3)   Child (of chosen gender)
    4)   Child (of chosen gender)

A happy gathering (FAMILY) of related, by choosing and by breeding, beings.
All together now, all together now, all together now...

or a family. (male/female edition)

    1)   Man (head)
    2)   Woman (heart)
    3)   Child (offspring of Man and Woman)

repeated as desired. Gender varies with description.

2.

Man/Woman become Husband/Wife become Gynophobe/Object

The man—the Prime Mover, gatherer of $Dollars$, consumer/source/sole decision source

POWER

(whereas and wherefore: over all others—house, progeny, family—all, subservient, power-less)

The woman—helpmeet, maid, servant, mother, cook, childcare, obedient, underfriended

THE DYNAMIC

a rooster, all puffed up feathers, crowing and angry (read: frightened) control

a hen, pecked until timid, obedient, rooster fearing, moving in smaller and smaller circles

3.

Once there was a man, uncomfortably anonymous the way silence can make a room blush. So went his days, one card at a time, one ticked atop another. And just as quietly and certainly, he became a door. Unlocked, undisturbed by bold paint, infrequently entered or exited. Became part of the apartment—its rooms, its progeny, its glass eyes, and settled into modesty and slow expectation. And so it was another Tuesday; the door, opened, breathing after several days, fastened to sleep and disinterested weather, when, like a rain-free rainbow, a hummingbird entered. At first shy, then in an echo-wing and click-song, residual images, mid-air constructions, a language of sound, movement, thought, becoming an alphabet, a community. But the hummingbird, threatened by an unfamiliar ease, grace-edged absent fear, flew away leaving its shadow. The door returned to its now-disturbed silence. Becoming a memorial to an absence, witness to dust's daily flirtation with friendless windows, seasonal calculations of light, approximations of grace, anything colour-hearted.

4.

15 years scorched off the calendar. Black curls of paper, billowy skeletons
from a fireplace. Archaeological remnants of a month-long conversation,
her side of the story. His, if somewhere, buried, ringed, convivial,
as solid as memory might be if in person.
Even looking back, what's possible less than water, breath, touch,
embrace – two bodies (nameless) coupled for a 12 second eternity
and then a continent or so, less hinged over time, less and less and nothing
save a parking lot, a few cars, a plate glass store window, caught winking again.

Rothko's Harvard Murals
(Sackler Museum—19th November 1986)

The immense murals were damaged from intense exposure to the sun. Their colors had gone from dark purplish-brown to "faded blue-jean."

Lee Seldes,
from *The Legacy of Mark Rothko*

Silence is so accurate.

*Phrasal somatic epiphany. Innocence-stripped atonement.
The soul, its contortions*

*perceptual, susurrated. Memory-scarred, recollected.
Transcendent, corporeal, autonomic. Disembowelled prayers.*

"A painting is not an experience. It is the experience."

Recipe for Art
(Mark Rothko, Lecture at The Pratt Institute, 1958)

A clear preoccupation with death—intimations of mortality.

Sensuality—Our basis of being concrete about the world.
(It is a lustful relationship to things that exist.)

Tension—Either conflict or curbed desire.

Irony—The self-effacement and examination.
(By which a man for an instant can go on to something else.)

A Library of Things
Mark Fleckenstein

Wit, play—The human element.

A few grams of the ephemeral and chance.

Hope.

"I do not believe that there ever was a question of being abstract or representational."

(The dark mood of the triptych was meant to convey Christ's suffering on Good Friday, and the brighter hues of the last mural, Easter and the Resurrection.)

"It is really a matter of ending this silence and solitude, of breathing and stretching one's arms again."

(What he wanted was a presence, so that when you turned your back to the painting, you feel that presence the way you feel the sun on your back.)

"I think of my pictures as dramas."

The past is simple; the present is difficult:
the future is even simpler.

Truth must strip itself of self.
A shadow looking back from the canvas.

One must go further, one must go further.
One must go first.

The result of my life is simply nothing —
the whole wall red.

Recipe Against Despair

> To truly not be in despair, you must at every moment destroy the possibility of being in despair.
>
> **Søren Kierkegaard**,
> from *Fear and Trembling Unto Death*

Begin with Bitterroot, Queen Anne's Lace,
the Deadly Nightshade, Pyrite, Autumn Dew,
Snap Dragons, Silkworm Cocoons. Crush
Tiger Lilies, Delphinium, Black Tulips,
four strands of her hair, one White Rose.

In a voice a soul freed as it breaks,
chant her name while stirring in Crabgrass,
Hyacinth, Chrysalis, Peyote. Calculate
the spectrum of rage from metal through mental.
Think of birds. Her face.

Crows, Sparrowhawks, Finches, Mourning Doves,
and Hummingbirds. Bring to rolling boil.
Fear living near Water, the Colour Red,
her Eyes, the Tilt of Last Night's Moon,
Telephone Calls like Half-Painted Rooms.

To rinse False Hope from the Room:
a Fingernail, Two Plastic Carnations,
a Family Portrait Photographed on Glass
and Painted. Burn them in Mercury and Recite
the Equation for Transmuting Lead into Gold.

If Despair continues, remove your Shirt.
Prick the Third Finger on your Left Hand.
Raise your Right Arm in Violence
against the Bedroom Mirror. Add Pearls
from a Broken Strand. Diagram the Heart's Motion.

Lamentation (1st Version)

> I can die now I just begun to live.
> **Charles Olson**

Misery loves what's left out:
dirty glasses, an argument

over new drapes, how to
compose a friendship.

No one comes out alive,
unscarred, content.

There's knowing and the door
the water glass tried to open.

The moon, close enough
to imagine someone's touch,

still, and will never answer.

Lamentation (2nd Version)

The beginning of doubt is the beginning of desire and life.
                                      James E. B. Breslin,
                                      Rothko: A Biography

Misery loves the torn white scraps
of shirt and gown, iridescent cloth

left by the dead any night
after familial wandering.

Daylight misquotes their thinking.

Lamentation (3rd Version)

At dawn he is still there, invisible, short of breath, mending his net
Charles Wright,
from "*Spider Crystal Ascension*"

Daylight misquoting torn white scraps
and shirts left by the dead

after familial wanderings. Night
upon night. Knotted, frayed thinking.

An unnecessary failure of red thoughts.

An Experimental Sonnet for Trump's America

This is no time for poetry, words dressed for dancing, awaiting the orchestra.
This is no time for light resembling a heart attack.
This is no time for panic, to tempt wrists to play bloody.
This is no time for right or wrong, induced arguments, plastic bags.
This is no time for imagining, stalling, starting, wondering how air is made.
This is no time for trees, giving both birth and abortion.
This is no time for misspelled remarks, U turns, memorizing disappearing light.
This is no time for assumptions, understandings, strangling soft beliefs.
This is no time for all the hands needed to build a city, a bridge, a week.
This is no time for numbers, looking for an unknown address, absent any light.
This is no time for painting pain neutral colours, memory, forgetting, starting over.
This is no time for surprises, shock and awe, the expectations for stars.
This is no time for joking, it's expensive, and only understood told backwards.
This is no time for poetry, words dressed for dancing, awaiting the orchestra.

A Near Sonnet with a Line by C.D. Wright

To be ashamed is to be an American.
To be ashamed is to explicate, then fuddle.
To be ashamed is to reverse engineer logic.
To be ashamed is to imagine you're right in several dimensions.
To be ashamed is to see a razor as a sign of forgiveness.
To be ashamed is a lost bag of hope and misspelled name.
To be ashamed is to believe a mirror's promises you killed.
To be ashamed is to lose your heart, freed soul, and still live.
To be ashamed is to wear the same skin, bruised and hateful.
To be ashamed is to be a line in the sand, crossed repeatedly.
To be ashamed is to believe truth is the same as power.
To be ashamed is to be a hero for many, many wrong reasons.
To be ashamed is to believe right and wrong are partners.
To be ashamed is to be an American.

Self Portrait from a Mirror's Perspective

How another year started: wore his clothes,
answered the phone, listened to music,

tried to read books, made conversation.
Language, always language, all his

invention. Door, book dust, fooled objects.
Heroically he holds a patched shadow!

Camus got it wrong, there's more than one
philosophic question—*what's next?*

The habit of one's-self—calamity,
artless, pretentious, preposterous.

The idea, photographed and missed most easily.

Self Portrait as a Twenty Five-Year Old Question

This night, that life, roped skin,
a generation between us.

Were you to pull or push enough,
stretch the umbilical lifetime

(breathing, bloodied, name-
battered, child tattered),

blood's remedy for flesh-mistakes.
The concept, a nine-week loss—

minor, human. Sky, an indifferently blue,
heart shriven, newly etched lines

of a face. Is God what's left?
25 years angry: not even words,

a scar-memory, frozen glass-like,
a concussion-like insult, shattered,

an end. Over, over, over, thinking,
thinking, thinking, unforgiven.

A thought like an aneurism, ignored as it ruptures.

Epithalamium (For Hannah and Kyle)

The hard math. One equals two equals one
equals *I'm here, I'm here, I'm here,*

the heart's song. Open, embraced, found.
Love as journey, not breathless, fraught,

or assumed. Hands curious, a graced moment.
Worlds improvised, essential, minus

language, misapprehension. Together, perfectly
and intimately gathered. A vow made flesh.

Made, not chanced. Intent, intention,
intentionally, and for each other.

No other words. Nothing else really matters.

A Library Of Things (Short Version)

When flowers whisper the secret of their fragrance,
what it would be if possible,

may that find you.

Notes

The Secret life of a Photograph

If you will know the correct order of letters,
you make a world, you make creation.
                    Don Delillo, The Names

make a line drawing
of everywhere you've ever lived,

and you'll end up drawing
your own face
           from the movie, The Dancer Upstairs

Partial Title Of A Photograph

The title of Francesca Woodman's photograph is:
"But lately I find a Sliver of Mirror is simply to slice an Eyelid"

Experimental Sonnet For Trump's America

The line, "This is no time for poetry" is from
C.D. Wright's poem, "Rising, Falling, Hovering"

A Near Sonnet With a Line by C.D. Wright

The line, "To be ashamed is to be an American" is from
C.D. Wright's poem, "Rising, Falling, Hovering"

About the Author

Mark Fleckenstein was born in Chicago, Illinois and grew up in Ohio, Connecticut, Michigan, North Carolina, and New Hampshire before settling in Massachusetts, after receiving his MFA from Vermont College.

Twice nominated for a Pushcart Prize, he has published four books of poetry: *Making Up the World* (Editions Dedicaces, 2018), *God Box* (Clare Songbird Publishing, 2019), *A Name for Everything* (Cervena Barva Press, 2020), and *Lowercase God* (Unsolicited Press, 2022); and three chapbooks: *The Memory of Stars* (Sticks Press, 1995), *I Was I, Drowning Knee Deep* (Sticks Press, 2007), and *Memoir as Conversation* (Unsolicited Press, 2019).

www.ingramcontent.com/pod-product-compliance
Lightning Source LLC
Chambersburg PA
CBHW020330010526
44107CB00054B/2047